Chameleons

By Erika and Jim Deiters

Raintree Steck-Vaughn Publishers

A Harcourt Company

Austin · New York
www.steck-vaughn.com

ANIMALS OF THE RAIN FOREST

Published by Raintree Steck-Vaughn Publishers, an imprint of Steck-Vaughn Company.

Library of Congress Cataloging-in-Publication Data
Chameleons/Jim Deiters, Erika Deiters.
p.cm.—(Animals of the rain forest)
Includes bibliographical references (p. 31).
Summary: Describes the habitat, physical characteristisc, and life cycle of chameleons, many of whom live in rain forests.
ISBN 0-7398-4681-7
1. Chameleons—Juvenile literature. [1. Chameleons.] I. Title II. Series: Animals of the rain forest.
QL666.L23 D45 2001
597.95'6—dc21

2001019509

Printed and bound in the United States of America
1 2 3 4 5 6 7 8 9 10 WZ 05 04 03 02 01

Produced by Compass Books

Photo Acknowledgments
Photophile/Robert Metzgus, 11
Visuals Unlimited/Jim Merli, title page, 22; Tom J. Ulrich, 6, 12, cover; Don W. Fawcett, 14; Joe McDonald, 16, 19, 20, 24, 26
Wildlife Conservation Society, 8

Content Consultants
Warren Paul Porter, University of Wisconsin

Maria Kent Rowell, Science Consultant, Sebastopol, California

David Larwa, National Science Education Consultant
Educational Training Services, Brighton, Michigan

This book supports the National Science Standards.

Contents

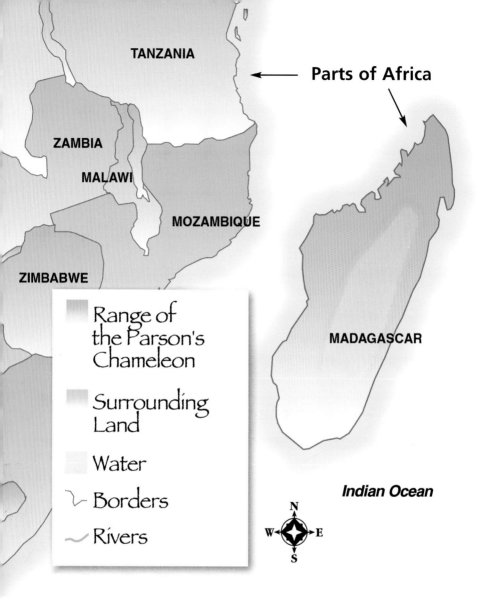

Parts of Africa

TANZANIA

ZAMBIA

MALAWI

MOZAMBIQUE

ZIMBABWE

MADAGASCAR

Range of the Parson's Chameleon

Surrounding Land

Water

Borders

Rivers

Indian Ocean

N
W   E
S

A Quick Look at Chameleons

What do chameleons look like?

Chameleons have long, flattened bodies. Their backs are high and rounded. They have large heads, and their eyes bulge. They are usually brown, green, or gray, and can change their colors in only a few seconds.

Where do chameleons live?

Most chameleons live in the rain forests of Africa and Madagascar. Madagascar is an island off the southeast coast of Africa. A few kinds of chameleons live in southern Europe and Asia, too.

What do chameleons eat?

Chameleons eat all kinds of insects, including grasshoppers, moths, dragonflies, caterpillars, and crickets. They lick dewdrops and raindrops from leaves when they are thirsty.

Chameleons live in rain forest trees.

Chameleons in the Rain Forest

Chameleons have been around since the time of the dinosaurs. The scientific name for the chameleon family is Chamaeleontidae (kuh-MEE-lee-uhn-TUH-day).

Chameleons live almost everywhere in Africa and Madagascar. Most live in the rain forest. Rain forests are warm places where many trees and plants grow close together and a lot of rain falls. They can also live in the dry sands of the desert or high in the mountains. A few **species** live in southern Europe and Asia. A species is a group of animals or plants most closely related to each other.

There are many trees and plants in the rain forest that provide food and shelter for chameleons.

▲ **Parson's chameleons are the largest of all the species of chameleon.**

Cold-blooded Reptiles

Chameleons are reptiles. A reptile is a **cold-blooded** animal that crawls or creeps. The body of a cold-blooded animal warms or cools to about the same temperature as the air or water around it.

Chameleons are lizards. Yet they are unlike other lizards. They cannot grow new tails. If other lizards lose their tails, most can grow a new one. Chameleons also move more slowly than other lizards.

Kinds of Rain Forest Chameleons

There are about 100 kinds of chameleons. About half live on the island of Madagascar. The Parson's chameleon is the largest chameleon. It can grow to almost three feet (91 cm) long. Other chameleons on the island are so small that spiders eat them.

The group of chameleons called stump-tailed chameleons are the smallest chameleons. They grow to less than one inch (2.5 cm). Stump-tailed chameleons live on the ground. They are gray and brown. Their color helps them blend in with the rain forest floor. Their feet are covered with small **scales**. Scales are pieces of hard skin that lay over each other. These help them grip the ground.

The Namaqua chameleon lives in Africa. It is also called the leaf chameleon. It looks like a dead leaf with a short stem. It is usually brown and has a short tail. It spends most of the time on the ground and is not as colorful as most chameleons.

Appearance

Chameleons have large heads. Their eyes bulge and are almost completely covered with skin. They can move each of their eyes in a different direction. One eye can look forward, while the other looks backward.

Chameleons have long, flattened bodies. Their backs are high and rounded. Their shape helps them balance on branches. Their shoulder blades move with their legs. This helps them reach farther out.

Chameleons have five toes on each of their feet. Their front feet have three toes on the inside and two toes on the outside. The toes on their back feet are opposite, with two toes inside and three outside. This allows them to grip things well. They also have sharp claws.

A chameleon has a prehensile tail that can be longer than the length of its body. They can wrap their tails around branches and hang from trees. They can also use their tails to grip branches as they climb. They roll their tails up to rest.

Male and female chameleons look different from each other. Males have thicker tails. They are also more colorful than females.

▲ **This chameleon has three horns on its head.**

Some kinds of chameleons have horns. They may have from one to four horns. Some have crests on top of their heads. A crest is a natural growth on the head of an animal.

All chameleons are covered with scales. They are made of a material called keratin. People's fingernails are also made of keratin.

▲ This chameleon's green color helps it blend in with plant and tree leaves.

Coloring

Chameleons are usually brown, green, or gray. Their normal color **camouflages** them. Camouflage is colors, shapes, and patterns that make something blend in with its background.

Sunlight, temperature, and mood make some chameleons change their color. They do not change color to hide, as many people believe.

When it is cold, their skin turns darker. Darker colors help them soak up the warm sunlight.

Chameleons turn tan if they are cold, sleepy, or sick. They turn yellow when they give up in a fight. When they are angry, they show bright colors. If they are very angry, they turn black.

Habitat

Most chameleons are **arboreal**. This means they live in trees. In a rain forest, the area of thick leaves and branches above the ground is called the **canopy**. The canopy provides a place to hide from predators. Predators are animals that hunt other animals and eat them. Chameleons sit still and use their usual coloring as camouflage to hide from predators.

Chameleons are not social. They like to live alone. They make their homes in different parts of the canopy. The canopy has lower, middle, and upper parts. Some chameleons like to live in the upper canopy, about 150 feet (46 m) above the ground. The lower and middle canopy are from 20 feet (6 m) to 100 feet (30 m) above the ground. Some chameleons live there. Others live on the ground.

▲ This chameleon has puffed itself up to look larger. It is ready to defend its territory.

What Is a Chameleon's Day Like?

Chameleons are active during the day. The warmth of the sun gives them energy. Their skin holds in the heat. Chameleons must be careful not to overheat. They cool off in the shade of the trees.

Chameleons rock back and forth when they move through the branches. This makes them look like leaves blowing in the wind. Moving in this way helps them hide from predators. It also allows them to sneak up on prey. Prey are the animals that predators hunt and eat.

Chameleons are **territorial**. A territorial animal lives on and fights to keep an area of land for itself. Chameleons defend their homes in the trees. They try to scare off other chameleons. They hiss, puff up their bodies, or show their teeth. They fight only if this show does not work.

Chameleons usually return to the same sleeping spot each night. They often sleep at the tip of a branch. This prevents a heavy predator, such as a leopard, from coming too close. A chameleon will even drop from a branch if it feels a predator's movement. It is able to quickly fill its body with air. This helps soften the fall. The puffed body floats if it lands in water.

This chameleon is hunting. Its tongue is curled in its mouth, ready to strike.

What Chameleons Eat

C hameleons are carnivores. Carnivores are animals that eat only other animals. Chameleons eat all kinds of insects, including grasshoppers, moths, and caterpillars. The trees where chameleons live are good hunting grounds.

Animals that eat insects must be careful. Some insects protect themselves with stingers and poison. The bearded chameleon, however, eats bees and does not get hurt. The Pardalis chameleon, too, is able to eat spiders that are poisonous to other animals. They do not make it sick.

Larger chameleons sometimes eat smaller lizards or other animals. The Meller's chameleon eats young birds. It takes them from their nests.

Chameleons lick dewdrops and raindrops from the leaves when they are thirsty.

How Chameleons Catch Food

To catch food, chameleons climb to a spot in the branches. They blend in with the rain forest treetops. Their prey cannot see them.

Chameleons sit and wait for their prey to come to them. Some place themselves among flowering trees and bushes. The flowers attract insects.

Chameleons have a poor sense of smell and hearing. But they can see very well. Chameleons can move their eyes separately in all directions to look for their prey. When the prey is close, chameleons point both eyes toward it.

Chameleons have long tongues. They pack their tongues in the back of their mouths. When they see prey, chameleons bring their tongues to the front of their mouths. They have a special tongue bone. It helps them aim their tongues at their prey.

Chameleons have two sets of muscles in their tongues. One muscle allows them to grab prey. The other muscle helps them pull their tongues back inside. In one-sixteenth of a second, they can shoot their tongues out and pull them back in.

The tip of a chameleon's tongue is rough and covered with sticky saliva. Prey stick to it.

This chameleon is eating an insect.

Chameleons have teeth on the rims of their jaws. They use their teeth to grind their food. A chameleon sits in the sun after it eats. The warmth of the sun helps it **digest** its food. The bodies of cold blooded animals digest food faster when they are warmer.

A chameleon can die if it becomes too cold after eating. The prey will rot in its stomach and poison the chameleon.

When a chameleon grows, it will shed its old scales so new skin can replace them.

A Chameleon's Life Cycle

Males become very colorful during the mating season. They use bright colors to attract females. Sometimes females will change color to show that they are not interested in the males.

Males also fight over females. These fights usually do not involve physical contact. Males puff up and hiss at other males to try to scare them away. The losing male turns darker green and walks away.

A male's face becomes red when he is ready to mate. The rims of his lips become yellow. The yellow lips are a sign to other males to keep away. The yellow is also a sign to females that the male is ready to mate. If a female is colored black with orange patterns, she is carrying young.

▲ **This female is digging a hole to bury her eggs.**

Eggs

Most chameleons lay eggs. The mother lays up to 50 eggs. She buries the eggs in the ground. Female chameleons leave after laying their eggs. They remain buried for several months. The eggs have many tiny holes that allow air and water to enter. The young chameleons breathe and drink while they are in the egg. They can die in the egg if the ground is too hot. They can also drown if the ground is too wet.

Young chameleons are able to stop growing inside the egg. This ability is called **diapause**. It allows them to wait for the right conditions before hatching. The ground has to be soft enough for them to crawl out of the buried nest. Once out, the young try to survive on their own.

Young

Chameleons never stop growing. They shed their skins as their bodies grow larger, just like snakes. They grow the most and shed the most during their first year.

Young chameleons are in great danger. Many animals of the rain forest prey on them. Young chameleons are usually gray or brown. These colors camouflage them against the trees. They can change color and puff themselves up. This makes them look larger. If they look larger, there is a better chance that smaller animals will be afraid of them.

Nobody knows how long chameleons can live in the wild. Scientists think they live for about two years. They have lived up to ten years under a scientist's care.

Without their rain forest habitat,
chameleons would die out.

The Future of Chameleons

Like many wild animals, chameleons are losing their **habitat**. The rain forests of Africa and Madagascar are disappearing. People are cutting down trees to make room for new homes and farms. They are also selling the wood from trees. Chameleons cannot survive without the forests.

Traders buy chameleons and sell them as pets. Chameleons, however, do not make good pets. When taken from the wild, chameleons usually die within a few weeks. That is because they need a certain amount of sun and certain temperatures to live. It is hard for people to create the conditions chameleons need to live.

This chameleon has wrapped its tail around the branch to keep from falling.

Did you know that many chameleons can hang from a tree branch by their tails? This is because chameleons have prehensile tails. These tails can grab things and wrap around them. They are strong enough to keep the chameleons from falling.

What Will Happen to Chameleons?

Some scientists are trying to breed chameleons to release in the wild. They are having a hard time. Only a few chameleons have been born.

Many people understand that chameleons are important to life in the rain forests. In some places, it is now against the law to sell or to remove them from the rain forests. Without laws, the sale and removal of chameleons from their habitats would probably increase.

Laws are not enough. People must make sure that the laws are obeyed. They must report people who break the laws. They must teach other people about the importance of chameleons. Laws and learning may help people keep chameleons alive in their rain forest homes for a very long time.

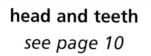

head and teeth
see page 10

eyes
see page 10

tongue
see page 18

sharp claws
see page 10

camouflage skin
see page 12

prehensile tail
see page 10

Glossary

arboreal (ar-BOR-ee-uhl)—living mainly in trees

camouflage (KAM-uh-flahzh)—colors, shapes, and patterns that make something blend in with its background

canopy (KAN-uh-pee)—a thick area of leaves high up in the treetops

cold-blooded (KOHLD BLUHD-id)—animals with body temperatures that change according to their surroundings

diapause (DIE-a-pauz)—an animal's ability to control its development within an egg

digest (dye-JEST)—to break down food so the body can use it

habitat (HAB-i-tat)—the place where an animal or plant usually lives

scale (SKAYL)—a small piece of thick, hard skin

species (SPEE-sees)—a group of animals or plants most closely related to each other in the scientific classification system

territorial (TAYR-i-tor-ee-uhl)—an animal that defends the land it has claimed as its home

Internet Sites

St. Zachary School's Rain Forest
http://www.mcs.net/~south/stdwrk.html

Tropical Rainforest Animals
http://www.ran.org/kids_action/animals.html

Useful Address

Rain Forest Action Network
221 Pine Street
Suite 500
San Francisco, CA 94104

Books to Read

Martin, James. *Chameleons: Dragons in the Trees.* New York: Crown, 1991.

Smith, Trevor. *Amazing Lizards.* New York: Knopf, 1990.

Index